Sometimes the feeling of fear overcomes, but let it go and it will transform your life.

Life is not living, you are alive, life is on its own.

Give me a good reason not to care, and I will literally give your freedom back.

Fear is nothing more than a wall in between something that we really want to stand for.

Every Materialistic Thing on our planet, is already yours, just work for it.

If you give up your dream, its the same as giving up your own life.

Don't see to believe. You must Believe then you will see. Then you be successful.

Konrad

HOPE

THE PERFECT PHILOSOPHY

KONRAD BUS

authorHOUSE®

AuthorHouse™ UK
1663 Liberty Drive
Bloomington, IN 47403 USA
www.authorhouse.co.uk
Phone: 0800.197.4150

Published by AuthorHouse 09/21/2015

ISBN: 978-1-5049-9086-8 (sc)
ISBN: 978-1-5049-9087-5 (hc)
ISBN: 978-1-5049-9088-2 (e)

HOPE

ARE we The Gods?

The Perfect Theory of Philosophy

Invitation to reality

Your Own Personal Letter for Reality

I want you to read this book in parts, so you have a time to think
it through and look at your own life from following perspectives.

This book is dedicated to all people who are lost with
their lives. This book is just about only little part of what's
the real life is about. I think and you should too.

What's wrong?

I'm sitting right here, thinking of what could happen if I only could break through and go out there, risk it. Life's hard. Life's easy. We cannot define life. Life is simply of it's own. How do you live every moment of life and try unstoppably becoming happy? What is happiness about? Do you know anyone who is happy in your life? Why are those people happy or why not? If somebody is unhappy, what's their reason? Is it really your life or is it actually our life? Are we the Gods Sons, and Daughters? Who is God? What is evil or my own ego? What is the whole point of our existence, what is the point of me being here? Do I need to work to live? Do I need to get up of my bed to live? Do I need to keep being abused and discriminated against because the will of other people? What's the real reason on being on this earth? Do you believe in angels? Who is devil, and what's his purpose? What is system we are living in? What's wrong with humanity? Why do religions fight with each other? The war is over, is there more to come? What's the

1

whole point? How is it to be awake? Life is easy and how do we prove its hardness? Why there is so much pain? Why do I get addicted to people, or other entertainment things? What does bible say about love? What do Jesus said about us? How our planet started with our form of life? Is there higher intelligence? Why do we study? Who is responsible for your life? Why we are slaves of our thoughts? Why do you hate and dislike? Where is my honour gone? Is life really that bad? Life seems the same everyday? Is there a problem at all, or you just think there is one?

It's time to get into work and find these
answers for every single question.

Why, why and why, because, because, because, sorrry, sorry, sorry, sad, sad, sad, should, should, sholud, won't, won't, won't, stop, stop!

You have to get our own life back, not the one you think you are in. I mean the real ONE!

Want to get started? Remeber that this book is not the book you NEED to believe in, my points, my own opinions and comments. Everything changes in life, and so we are too.

Back to reality, or maybe it's just a bad dream?

"Everything that we see is real. Why, nobody ever told us that we could be happy and live the never ending dream on this star in the universe? The star is called earth. And it's just a normal planet. With dumbed people in it. Why there is no explanation to this question or the facts? What if there is an actual answer, but it has been hidden from us? Let's look at this.

Once you get born, you go through life as a slave. Your entire life you are working and going through your life as a slave. People are lying to them selves assuming that everything is real, that they are totally free and they have freedom from harm in their lives by working for many, many corporations and are not getting anything out of their own life's. Are you sure about that? I am writing about a person just like you. How many things did you want to do in your life, but you haven't done anything because of fear? Look how much fear we have got in our world that is tortured, destroyed by wars, people hypnotized to negative thinking and harmed through their own subconscious minds. Our world and our lives are manipulated all the time without any break. So, if you want change to rewire your mind and be born once again, you will need to give up worries and attachements and die, to be reborn.

So, when society is being told a lie, and everyone is talking about it. They are talking about it for so long that most of people start to believe in that lie, they drag in more and more others in it. After short period of time, a lie will develop its fundamentals to create the fake truth. This is how our minds work. If you have been told that you cannot achieve anything in your life when you were little, you go through life believing somebody's opinion. But, because this is only an opinion of someone believe system and it is really only an opinion, then it should be considered as a lie. You cannot listen to other people telling you what you need to do with your life, even if that's your parents. Your life is of your own. You have been created to go through pain, start something big in your life which should influence more people. We all should live together without arguments or wars. But, no. We had to be separated by others. When we were young our parents started to show and say things in their own way, the way they see life. They were simply lying to us without knowledge that they do it anyway. This is not their fault. But, what if they were already lied to, what if you have been given a training when you were young to see world as a beautiful place, to run away from pain, to keep your head down and work until you retire. That's what they told you. They have been lied by their own parents, their parents have been lied by others and now it's your turn to be lied to.

When you are lied to, you go to school and you taste abuse, bullying, stupidity, dumbness and negative thoughts, negetive thinking, your faults and mistakes pointed out! This teaches you fear, this makes you paralysed, and you cannot break free from your own head. You are getting into this ego mind, deeper and deeper until it has control over you. Your own emotions are lying to you! This lie and sense of fake truth is taking its own initiative at a point when you give up your life. This is called selling your soul to the devil. Believe or not, life is hell and it always have been the same. Life is hell, but in order to get out of it you need to start working on your self. Develop, learn, mentally die every single day, get depressed and one day you will feel freedom and redemption. Redemption won't last too long as you are living in this hell everyday. Devil wants your soul, God wants your soul too. You create your own life, and nobody should be able to do it for you. Remember that this is hard path but, it is more important than living in total darkness all the time. Think about your life right now, and say to your self how do you feel about your self, what you lost and what you want. Say to your self that you have literally enough of going though life as a victim. Remember that you are the most powerful thing in the universe, you are nothing and you are everything. See your self as a person who has a mission which has been taken away from you many years ago and you are not happy at all with your current life. Hate your life, it doesn't mean to commit suicide at all, but to embrace it so the pain you get back, will push you through the tough moments. Suicidal won't help as you will go to hell due your sins you haven't repaired or you just comeback to the earth once again as a different person, with different perspective, but your won't remember your past life. This is only an perspective of being receiranated. This might be just a lie still, but nobody really knows if there is life after death. Live your life to the fullest, now. It's easy to die, but it's hard to live. Let me tell you something. It is better to die trying and turn your back away from religion, towards our only God, than just commit suicide and not experience the rest of your life. It will be better to go through life in pain and help people around you than just give up and miserably pull a rope around your neck. Do you want that? The people who trust you and belive in you, embrace and love at some point of their life will suddenly loose your smiles, happiness, tears and commitments, bad situations and the better ones, and most importantly "YOU"!

At the beginning of your life, you should be told that your life is just a game. So, which level are you at this moment? If you don't know, you need to start your life once again. This would be the only way, to get free. Leave your surroundings, and the people in that area. Sacrifice everything and become nobody. You will need to die, to become nobody. How do I die if I need to keep on living? The reason why you need to die is because, in order to find your true purpose in life you have to be a child. Why were you thinking that life is just another dream? If you said no you are wrong. Life is a dream, but it has been constructed in a specific way that we don't even recognise it. This is a simulation of your own mind, you feel love, pain, disappointment, angry, good, happy, competitive, defensive only by your own mind, mind which have been manipulated for most of your life through teaching, learning, asking, talking, experiencing, and believing people who are wrong in their own way. Negative, naive and trying to lie, so this lie is taking over their minds, so they are starting to fake their life without knowing about it. If a person is trained to go to work and concentrate on their work, how much they like it or hate it, they will look at this work as the only thing in their life. Because of that, they miss everything else. They miss the reality which is blinded by their own thoughts, opinions of others, entertainment, food, drinks, sex or TV and news. These people are called brainless, idiots, dumb or zombies. You need to really see this things the way they are, instead of looking into one thing at a time. Talking of time, it simply doesn't exist. Of course, that the past and future of the universe exists but, the time on our planet doesn't exist at all. It has been created by some other person in the same illusion of this simulation. It has been created to define day and night, but it has been used against people of our planet. But now, even if the time doesn't exist on the earth, it has been invented anyway right? Now, we just need to use it in the right way. Every hour, minute, and seconds within the 24 hours each day, how you use it? It only depends on you and your own thoughts, actions, situations, assertivenes and confidence. If you don't believe in yourself, you won't do anything great even after mistakes and failures. Why you ask? Without small courage and without believing in yourself you will simply give up and stop asking for more pain and fears to challenge. On the other side of our fear, is the person you need to be and it is essential you to become.

What is life in it's true colours? Have you been told that live is not about this realistic life that we see, but the spiritual war. Spiritual war is the biggest truth you could ever hear about. God is love and he wants your soul back, Evil is money, singful sex, entertainment, and wars only to keep you away from the truth that God really exist. Your life has been manipulated in thousand different ways. Through matrix on the streets, when you are working towards paychecks, Tv's, news and dumb belifs of other people.

In the beginning there was blackness, God said for the light to appear, light appeared. This is our life. Once you get born and you live on the dark side of the world with people who see, but are blind, with people who hear but, are deaf. This is why it is necessary to break free out of the mental slavery.

My question is as follows: "Who are YOU right now?" and the next question is: "Who do YOU want to BECOME?"

If you don't realise that you are GOD of your own, you won't make your life better. What did I say? How can I be a God? Yes, nobody will ever do anything for you, only you can do it! Only you can succeed and you are creating your life even now! DO NOT WAIT FOR SOMEBODY TO HELP YOU, JUST BECOME BETTER AND LEARN FROM **your successes**!

Once you were born, you haven't have an TV, you haven't have a car, or guitar, house, or anything that belongs to you because it wasn't yours. It was your parents who brought it and then shared it with you. It wasn't yours. When you were a baby, you did not care if there was somebody to be with you, you didn't love, hate, speak, you haven't own anything. You were nobody until you were given a name. A name is the first attachment you get in life. Then when you grow up, and if you even hate your name you will go through life miserable, unsatisfied, unhappy and a victim. But there is the truth. You are attached to the things you have or own, and this is true. The things you are attached to, own you and not the other way. Imagine your self as a person without anything. Do you feel good or bad, or nothing and why? The answer is interesting. If you feel good, you are probably still attached to something, if you feel bad, you are terribly attached to something, but when you are feeling nothing at all and you just live in this nature, you are free. In this moment when you are feeling nothing, you are more than the things you owned, people you speak to, you are the creature of this earth, you don't need or ask for anything. You feel that you have it all. I don't need a party, coffee, tea, food, work, tv, newspapers, mobile phone or negative people around my life and even my own name. This is time when you experience death, because when you were born and when you die that's only two moments in life when you are totally free from worries or anything a path from life it self. You become your self again, as when you were a baby. Once you die due a pain which should be embraced as much as possible, you become mentaly free. Nobody will ever convince you to anything because you have your very own mind again.

Why all of this is happening here? If we a virtually created by someone's mind, and this life is only an event of being in a dream in somebody's mind, then why we have got wars and all of these disappointing situations around the globe? The truth is real but, also always fake. There are only few people in the world that know the real truth, there are also people who think that they know the truth but, they are also wrong. People, who do believe anything in what they read or say, to them all opinions are normally just like a food to their brains. But, look how powerful are you. Your life is all about being all the best, better than anyone else, wasting your life and entire time for things that you don't really need at all, making life a disappointing adventure. What's your purpose in life?

Do you really think that life is just another dream? If you said no you are wrong. Life is a dream, but it has been constructed in a specific way that we don't even recognise it. This is a simulation of your own mind, you feel love, pain, disappointment, angry, good, happy, competitive, defensive only by your own mind, mind which have been manipulated for most of your life through teaching, learning, asking, talking, experiencing, and believing people who are wrong in their own way. Negative, naive and trying to lie, so this lie is taking over their minds, so they are starting to fake their life without knowing about it. If a person is trained to go to work and concentrate on their work, how much they like it or hate it, they will look at this work as the only thing in their life. Because of that, they miss everything else. They miss the reality which is blinded by their own thoughts, opinions of others, entertainment, food, drinks, sex or TV and news. These people are called brainless, idiots, dumb or zombies. You need to really see this things the way they are, instead of looking into one thing at a time. Talking of time, it simply doesn't exist. Of course, that the past and future of the universe exists but, the time on our planet doesn't exist at all. It has been created by some other person in the same illusion of this simulation. It has been created to define day and night, but it has been used against people of our planet. But now, even if the time doesn't exist on the earth, it has been invented anyway right? Now, we just need to use it in the right way. Every hour, minute, and seconds within the 24 hours each day, how you use it? It only depends on you and your own thoughts, actions, situations, assertivenes and confidence. If you don't believe in yourself, you won't do anything great even after mistakes and failures. Why you ask? Without small courage and without believing in yourself you will simply give up and stop asking for more pain and fears to challenge. On the other side of our fear, is the person you need to be and it is essential you to become.

What is life in it's true colours? Have you been told that live is not about this realistic life that we see, but the spiritual war. Spiritual war is the biggest truth you could ever hear about. God is love and he wants your soul back, Evil is money, sinful sex, entertainment, and wars only to keep you away from the truth that God really exist. Your life has been manipulated in thousand different ways. Through matrix on the streets, when you are at work or paychecks, Tv's, news and dumb beliefs of other people.

In the beginning there was blackness, God said for the light to appear, light appeared. This is our life. Once you get born and you live on the dark side of the world with people who see, but are blind, with people who hear but, are deaf. That's why it is necessary to break free out of the mental slavery.

My question is as follows: "Who are YOU right now?" and the next question is: "Who do YOU want to BECOME?"

If you don't realise that you are GOD of your own, you won't make your life better. What did I say? How can I be a God? Yes, nobody will ever do anything for you, only you can do it! Only you can succeed and you are creating your life even now! DO NOT WAIT FOR SOMEBODY TO HELP YOU, JUST BECOME BETTER AND LEARN FROM **your successes**!

Mr Nobody

My name is Nobody, I have nothing at all, but also everything that I needed to have. My story has been dark but, when I become one light and enlighten more people, I am free. How did this happened? I'll tell you my story.

My mother raised me up with her warm hands, she finally have her son in her arms. Holding to me tightly. Her green eyes started to shine in happiness and that smile on her face is priceless. Everything is so great and beautiful for her. Father just came into the hospital room to see us together and he started crying, although I knew I am the best thing that happened in their life. Once I have been born, both have agreed to give me a name, a attachment that will last me until I die, then they booked me into society book only to give me a number on a paper. This is time where they sell me to a corporation, to a big massive banking system. I started to grow up and within time started to make my life even more disgusting every single next day, it was worse and worse. I have blond hair, green eyes and strange dyslexic disability which I have not known about before I was about twelve years of age. I couldn't learn, dream, think under pressure, make clear decisions at any time, got into trouble everyday. Everything was horrible, and also I've been called different names as I have never told anybody about my illness, more of them called me mentally ill or just lazy and dumb. I kept this issue on my mind a total secret. I have never told anybody about it. When things got hard, I started to blame everything on me and everything around, I was stupid to do that. But, who knew that this will be the best thing that ever happened to me. This means, I was always at the point where I needed to be, when I didn't then there was that mechanism I my brain that made me miserable, scared and unconvinced about my situation. This has been a good indication to change my circumstances, and so I did.

I always had a problem with standing up to people. I didn't want to hurt their feelings, no matter how bad they were to me. I know that what ever they thought of me, it wasn't them, but their ego. Life is hard and no matter how much I tried to do anything it never worked, but I never gave up on anything. If I failed on something, I always tried it again. But never gave in. How do you go through life with lots of disappointment and worries around. It is almost impossible. But, tell me. What is impossible with God? The answer is nothing. And I am nothing. Once you become nothing, you are everything, and the same is with God. Believe God and really give your life to him and this is the only way to feel free, and against will of Satan's work on other people. These people are blind and the only way to feel free is to totally feel something that is real. You need to go through pain, to feel you are alive. If you think that after having beer one day and every other you will feel good, you are right because society told you a lie. You need to understand that Society is wrong, mainstream media is killing our mind from good to depressed and worse. Find God and allow God to find you. Once you do that you will feel depressed, you will get new ideas on how to kill fear, and it will be hard, it will be challenging, you will feel like you are going to cry now and then, you will go through disappointments.

It is important not to be better than anyone else, but being your self. The way you have been created, the way you hold yourself. Be angry, furious and totally disappointed with your life because it is seemingly out of any sense. Working for a system where nothing is real, and is turning your way away from freedom, from fulfilment. Keep on the track for what you need, don't listen to nobody's opinions because your life is yours. Your life is only the way you create it, and God has a plan for you, it is painful, full of fears and tears, he will tell you how to survive. Don't see life as bad when you loose your money or love, because it is only attachment which is in your mind. Now, look at your life from a third perspective. The way you would see your self, with somebody else's eyes. You are here and you are looking at your self from different perspective. What do you see in your self? Sadness, happiness, lovingness, fears, disappointment, aggressiveness or fake you.

And What Now?

I woke up once again, with tears in my eyes. What can I do to stop thinking and start doing? I have read lots of different books, I have been preparing for this time to change my life all over again. But, again I've woke up crying to the pillow and cannot do anything with my life, I am alone. Nobody understands me, and I don't understand anybody. How can you live your life with being a fake person. People don't realise how much they are wasting every day on their live going to work, and surviving only to pay tax or debt. They are buying things they don't need only to feel happy. But, how long does that happiness last? One day, two days, month or a year? Is this really what we need to be happy? To buy new stuff every two months to keep our self entertained. Is it not better to see the world, to have sense of adventure. To have a dream to live life to its full potential, than look at people living their dream on the TV screen. I hate this life I'm in, and that is the misreable life. Looking at a TV screen, watching news of people getting paid huge amount of money only for being free due to their values. Why cannot I be just Like THEM? Why? Becuase I am me, Im different, I have different values, different dreams and thats why I'm still not there. Still, One day I make it anyway!

Now I got up and went to work. Again in so many years, I'm at work. And I cannot see any point of wasting entire day only to be in one place, do the same thing again and again only to feel that I hate it after a while. And again I missed live because I went to a place where my soul have been taken by them, money and reputation created by the same system. Schooling system, what's the point? They want you to pay money, and learn things that you need to remember than teach how to really understand the life the way it is.

How do I get to feel free, and keep on living and working in this stupid life? What if I change my mental system? Turn my self to God and become a warrior. Warrior of my own life. I want a level, in which nobody will ever convince me that I am less than them. I am the same as they are, but more with my soul once I turn towards God."

Love

Love is the strongest and the most important feeling in the whole universe. That is because you by feeling good on the planet send reaction to universe and this will bring a change to other people too, same way you are changing. How do they change? Say for example, you are getting out of your bed, miserable of waking up on Monday morning and you NEED to go to work. You have to go to work because the bills NEED to be paid, and you NEED warm water, you NEED internet and television working to keep your self entertainment. What's the point? Television doesn't give you anything but, stupidity and disturbing mind setting which enables you to hate yourself. To be fair most of the people don't know what they are, who they are and what's their purpose. Life is beautiful once you are aware. And once you are aware you will be depressed like never before. You will see stupidity of other people, how they are coping with their childish anger. Lots of them stopped growing when they reached 5 years old.

How an elderly kid will know that he wasted his life time? Maybe because on his death bed when he still reminds on what he has not done, once he was young. But, what is love really about? Is it, being nice to people or even becoming sexual interested in somebody. No! You have it all wrong. This is exactly what the soaps and TV entertainment is trying to do with your head. You are blind. When was the last time you thought of God to ask him why he doesn't give you what you want? If you want to change and feel the real love then drop everything. Sacrifice you computer games, playing time and consoles, TV and radio time, even your cell phone. You need a change, and once you will feel like you lost everything you will feel depressed. This is hard, real hard to do to sacrifice everything. Think about what will happen if you do it. You will feel depressed. This is important feeling that will make you feel painful inside.

Actually let me tell you the truth. You haven't ever have your own life until you have computer, games or tv on which you might be addicted already. You are being your tv, so it is essential that you forget everything that you seen on it or even remembered something that will never help you. That would be a stage where you will try to defeat EGO. There is many types of being depressed in this world and we haven't got a living until we sacrifice things you enjoy or love to find the real you. This kind of depression is different as it get its attention, you will feel weak and this is a good thing. You are alive, and until your heart is pulsing you have to feel fear, pain and bad in order to become confident and sure on what you want out of you. Your life is about to destroy the old you, and become the same person with different behaviour, with gaining more experience, skills. It is not easy, but it is actually very hard. It takes awfully long period of time, but it is worth it. Worth every minute, second. If it was easy everybody could do that, everybody could change. Your mentality is your only power. Your fear is a motivation to destroying all the figures and information that are destroying you from inside. Love is fear, love is kindness and willing to help. Love is not sex date, its not one night stand. You just making a prostitute of your self. People will tell you it's normal, no its not. Nature is smarter that humans are.

Once you have something or someone, nature will take it away from you just to make you aware of how much you need this thing or this person. Real love doesn't have problems which would destroy relationship. Until you don't stop judging other people, and making fun out of them. You will still be imprisoned by your self. Actually, it is not you who created bad feelings in your mind, but EGO. If your are thinking like a kid and don't become depressed, you will never grow. Why? Because in order to grow, you need pain. Pain will lead to Love, a very strong love. You have to accept people that they are dying, they have one day or 60 years before they die. It doesn't matter. They are dying, and once you know you are seeing them only for some period of time, there has to be a place for love. You are dying too. Remember this. Life is not a Movie, when you have a chance you take it, people are constantly becoming alive once again then they die again, you are here, so you can change. If you were in a movie, you could do anything because you are the main character. E.G Superman. Think about it this way. There are hard times hitting us straight in our faces, but how would you feel to get hit and do nothing about it. This is what you probably doing right now, taking no action what so ever. But, if you were a SUPERMAN, how would you feel, talk, stand, create a reaction, showing confidence or building self esteem. No body is perfect in what they are doing, every one is getting into hard times and make mistakes, but it's all about what you get from that. So what's love has to do with it? You need to create a new person, the very new and fresh you. You are the best and the smartest person on the earth and you are willing to do anything to achieve you goal without thinking negatively, overcoming short-cuts and obstacles. Still, what love has to do with this? I tell you. A lot. If you find something what you love then you will find out also a way to do it all the time, if you love other people more than you love yourself, you are dead and in very deep sleep. Life is about you. Once you find you, you will be able to truly love others. Remember!

Pain and Work

How many people wish to go back to school these days, most of them are 30 years old and find out that they have been wasting they life. The reality is that life has something to give, but in order to get it, we need to invest something first. It can be a smile, flowers, words of appreciation, helping somebody, give them clothes, new shoes or food with drink, time developing new skills or even being alone and creating new path in your mind. No, money isn't important at all. Money have been created in the system to show who's wining and who's loosing in the game. We are slaves, without rights. Police assume they have more privilege over us than we have over our life. They really have more rights against you, only because government wanted this to happened. People talk behind your back, talk to you in a foul way, they hate you for who you are so what you need to do? Fake it. Well, it's not right to fake your self at all, but if you are afraid you will. It's not right to fake, instead with a consequence show them that you are here, that your life has a value.

Somebody in the past said that you need to "Get Mad!", and don't point finger at people when you didn't get somewhere in your life because of this person or someone else.

If you are a failure, the truth is that you have created it. But, that's great if you are an failure and you see it already, if you addmit to it straight away. That means that your Ego pride is loosing with the strength of your true self. It's never too late to turn things around. That is great when you are depressed, and do not fight it. Depression will encourage lots of thoughts about depression and self doubt, but you understand that depression is being a failure. Not exactly. Because depression is a word only to describe your feeling. This feeling is given to you. I believe that when someone is depressed, God is trying to show that something is not right in your personal life. Then you need to start something new, create new path in your life, leave addicted situation, move forward, start learning and create. Anthony Robbins once said that small changes create big results. Pain, when is overcoming you and you have enough how the things are turning out in life. This disappointment is essential for you to snap and say "Enough, I will not live like this any more." This means that you cannot stop now and keep on working on your dream because you will give higher percentage into your work. The consequence of your bad decisions made you to loose yourself, and you are responsible to what's going on in your life. But, first prove this to yourself.

If you find out that something is not right in your life, then find a way to make sure that this will be an important step in your life to deal with. To find your self once again, you have to go through a lot of pain. What is pain? Pain is a feeling which you can defeat unless it's long-term physical, you need to wait until it disappears. Mentally if you feel bad that means there's something wrong, and it's your mind set. Everything is fine, it is you who create trouble, problems, excuses, anger and any other feeling to your self only in your mind. Unless, you are aware of your surrounding which can be harmful to becoming yourself. The only feeling that you really want in your life is love as it is the only sense of real life. To start working on your self, make a plan or not. Every one is different but, we are all the same. The differences are only in the mind.

You can make a plan of the day and do everything on the list. Then feel good while doing it, feel happy. Think happy. When the happiness will overflow you, the next day you might feel terrible or even better than last day. Set your self a goal that you are afraid of, and this could be a call to somebody, just pick up the phone and don't think of anything, but feel good. If you feel bad and you loosing it, just get the guts and say "I won't allow my fears to take over my life" and dial the number. This is an example on how to deal with anxiety. Start somewhere and build your way into more and more advanced things. You will see after a while that you don't need to fear anything because you already did this many times before.

If I hear a complaint or a judgement, I don't care because you don't know me. I don't have to care, because if you are thinking that I'm stupid then you are right, but only in your mind. You have been programmed to feel negative to others. I am my self, me is I. I love my self. The work of going through all the pain is to finally to understand ourselves. To find the meaning of our life and make sure that me is only me and I am always the same. If you want to love, love your self first. You won't spread your love across to others if you feel bad about your self to begin with. Become lonely, feel fear, feel bad, feel sad, feel depressed and sacrifice everything to become nobody. Once you are nobody and you went through so much pain, you will get up one day and you will be stronger as ever before. You will be able to do things that you were afraid of doing in the past. Once you are nobody, you can't be broken, you can't be anxious, you are wonderful being with out fear. Then build your relations with other people. What feeling do I need to use? Of course the feeling is Love.

At this point I want you to take a big breath and feel it with your heart. Make a decision that what ever you need to go through in life, you will never ever give up. Say it out loud!

I HOPE you enjoy this journey through higher self.
Now take 10 minutes break, then carry on
reading, there is much more to come!

Talk to yourself

Positive meaning, and feeling and words are influential on our well being. Feel something that will go through your mind for the whole day, something that really has a meaning to your life. I don't have examples because this is individual thing to have different interests. Everything is good, and your life is totally fine. If you feel bad and unaware of your life at any point of it, don't give up. Try to keep going because this is going to be the biggest obstacle if you give up on your dreams at any moment. You should do everything to your potential and intellectual purposes to grow. When you grow, and your life has a meaning you will see that you will become something different than the losers surrounding your life. So, feel good and never give up. Love your work, because it will be to be your biggest step in your life. Your entire life is based on work, and now decide if you want to work for somebody or you want to make your dream become a reality, and become something more than just a slave of your thoughts. Just make a plan and follow it.

It's still very hard and it doesn't matter how many hours you will waste on each thing from that list you create out of your planning. Even with a failure you need to be aware that this new life experience will destroy you or will make something greater out of it. Just make sure you do it everyday forward. If you need to dance, take a dance lessons. If you need to shoot from a big gun then ask somebody to show you how to do it. Attend gym and stop being afraid with people watching you if that's the case. Be strong and make sure you will be yourself. If you don't know who you are then you need to make a step in this direction to find your self. You will find out how long you can stay lonely and alone, how tough you are, how the mind of your thoughts is working and what you are AFRAID of. Take the chance to make sure you will find what ever you need in your life. Maybe you want to be a professional doctor, nurse, actor, sales man, or create something great according to your personal goal to encourage people to follow. Whatever your dream is, be competitive to yourself only, show and prove to yourself that you are the one. You have value in your life, you are the person who will fail more than thousand times to become somebody, who will succeed once. Fail more than thousand times only to success once!

Every fail you will go through will destroy you or make you stronger so, it is important to make sure that everything you go through, you are using right and positive mind set, determination and will power. Listen. I know it's strange but once you have been in hell for so many years you will see the change after first failure. Don't be afraid and never try to remember past performances. But, instead, do not be happy or satisfied with your past performances, in order to grow. There are lots of evil obstacles in the way of process of becoming who you want to be or working on your dream, only to make you stop. We are excusing our selves with saying that the devil is so strong and that's why we carry on doing wrong. What? When devil is too strong you give up? Never!! Remember that you can always be on Gods side if you believe that God is really in you, he is making you walk, he gives you good ideas. So, feel good and that will enable you to be more with God.

Your life is totally bad and miserable. You have lots of friends and no body even cares for you. This is the life you wanted? Smoking, drinking alcohol and poisoning yourself when you can actually grow! Leave the old you and become aware, you will not like it at the beginning, but if you want to see a value in your life you will purpose until you succeed. If you are the same, if you feeling bad about your life this means that you haven't sacrifice your life to anything. You don't grow, you don't develop the skills you have. Now, if you don't believe in your self then you are depressed. And that's good. Feeling of being depressed is good, that makes you think of what you could do better, so what's the problem? Now I want you to get up off your ass, and shout out loud the reason why you are an failure! Get up and shout out loud this "Me...name.., is a total failure and in order to do anything with my life I need to STOP

BEING LAZY! MY LIFE HAS A VALUE!" From now on you will feel anger, and amazement. Then you might cry and it's a sign that you will change. Think positive, feel positive, do positive, speak positive and fight to get your real life back!!

What's the real problem?

People are often doing things that they think they are doing right, but there is always somebody to prove them wrong and his also right, but only in his own mind. Everyone is the same with different brain and mind setting. This is because the system we are living in is teaching us things that we shouldn't even know about, ever. In the "perfect" world which existed 6000 years ago. People were free, they were real men, they had everything they wanted, they were happy and living in peace. Then something happen. Devil was so strong to make his allies. The men of devil started to make prisoners throughout the ages of times. These people are now called the government. Back then they started to use people to build, and started to taking over the world. All of these battles in the world were only because in order to take the over state was to kill all of the offenders and rebels. The problem is the evils work, but God wanted this to happened. This is a test to our will, to test our lifes and test our souls. We should treat others with respect, never being afraid, curious, contagious, bad, mad, sad, angry, and many more bad feelings, in the perfect world.

Why? Because it destroys you. If you think you are cool, smart or stupid. You are right, but only in your mind. Beware of the Ego. Learn about being neutral in your life, don't be happy to a praise, don't be angry to a problem. It's just there, this problem is just there. Where? In your head. Think about it. Problems don't exist until you call it to be. Nothing happens in the world of your life to you if you are not creating it. Remember that you are on this earth and you have a meaning to be a small part of us. If you don't change and there is much less people that are actually changing at all, then better stay at home and cry. If you get guts and fight for your freedom to help others, it has a meaning. You are really here to make a difference. Have you ever read bible? If you haven't don't worry. You don't have to, just remember lessons of love and appreciation Jesus told us about towards other people.

If you don't believe it then become aware of your self. Sometimes it takes 6 years to become aware sometimes 10 or 20. But once you become aware you will see your life in colours, you will have a different concept and totally different better and clear point of view. Something that you have, in reality you haven't have this thing. The change path is real hard and this will be the hardest thing in your entire life, but because it is so hard, that means it is the most benificial.

You just don't own nothing

Nothing belongs to you. You have nothing,. Just imagine you have the best console, computer, tv, mobile phone and Lamborghini at a beautiful house. One day you take a holiday for a week time and you leave everything behind, you have took a taxi to drive you to the airport. The flight you have taken was to Spain and you spend a week time there. You went to the beach, you had the best drinks and sun everyday. Your life is amazing and you have everything. On the last day you are packing your bags and suddenly have a message in your email box that your bank withdrawn all your money to somebody that you don't know. You have a flight back to your country, then a drive at your house. When you are near your house, from the taxi door window you see open front door of your own house. You're in shock and get angry. You get out off the taxi, and walk into the front door of your house and you see nothing. Everything is gone. Totally everything. You see white painted walls. No beds, furniture, any of your documents, any of consoles, tvs and so on. You are not having a thing. You get out of the house and cannot see your car anywhere. How do you feel? Sad, angry or intimidated? Or maybe happy, cool and totally fine because you had the best week off this year. You have went to your friend to ask for the bedding. He is happy to give to you, and you are going back to your empty house. You put everything on the floor and sleep. The next day you are waken by the police banging in the door. You get up open the door in hope they want to help you, and maybe they knew what happened. No. they are here to get you out of the house because it has been sold 3 days ago. And you starting to laugh or cry? You don't own nothing, and now your life is suddenly empty. If that didn't happen to you, then you cannot say that you have a problem in your life. So, stay positive and feel the happiness. When you worry, you just creating double amount of disappointment. So is there a problem? Yes, but only if YOU create it. Other ways, no, because things are the way they are.

A higher intelligence

Do you believe in aliens? No? Why? Universe is huge. There are thousands of planets with creatures just like us or totally different. Think about it. If you are a small human on our planet then you are actually living in the universe. People tend to forget that we are the planets animals. We humans are the animals, and not matter what you think, it is only the system that enslaved you to create different way of thinking about your own life. If there are aliens in the space somewhere out there then why do they don't communicate with us. Well, if you also think they don't communicate with humanity, then you cannot be more wrong than you are. How do I know? Because the secret agents won't ever say anything about the most secret creatures visiting our planet. There has been many times where people have seen a UFO but they didn't know that government will make a problem out of this only to hide the truth. They are trying to put you into wrong direction so we as public will never find out the real intentions of the other life forms.

People make stupid supposedly funny jokes about aliens but, they don't believe in their existence. It's the same way as saying that they will never die, because they don't believe. Please, don't be out minded. Be aware on what's going on in the world. We are controlled by governments, which is actually borrowing so much money that the public debt is getting higher. One day there will be a total destruction to the market it self and not only government will ask to pay everything that people have to pay the debt. So, lets ask a question relating to the topic. Are we not a alien to ourselves. I don't understand why there is so many people living without the brain. They go to work or shopping everyday, they work for somebody that really don't really care for them. They just want their money. This person is an alien, because in our mind you don't know this person or even his intentions. This is exactly the same with the aliens of outer space. There are theories about 6 or 7 gods from different planets. These gods have came to our earth planet once it has started to live. Then they created us to enslaved us to dig for gold. Funny?

The totally strange story might be true. So, they came on to our planet to create a new type of creature. The creatures are us. But many millions years ago, these "us" looked totally different or similar to us until now. Through the generations there were tests created on humans to see if a super human can be created. This has included many of experiments starting with mixing up the genes, to transplanting up the body parts to change the genes in humans. Psychology was probably the most important thing we could ever establish to learn about. Many people are inspired by the mind and brain working in order to change a human behaviour. So, yes. Aliens exist if you want it or not. But what about God or Evil?

Religion Wars and Avoidance

Which God do you believe in?

Because on our earth we have got two Main Gods that everyone knows about, but there is also nobody to believe in the people's change to their conscious minds. We have The Lord God and The Devil called Satan or Lucifer. Remember that they are both real and fighting against each other all the time, also, they are fighting for our souls. Stand guard at your truest self.

God has created our planet, and in the bible it is said that God created everything including Adam and Eve. Yes, God has actually created everything natural on our planet. Plants, trees, animals, humans and other creatures in the universe. Now, God is something more than universe. Think about it. Say for example, if the only way to get to God is though Jesus then, Jesus is the universe. God has to be something more, and this is why people don't believe in God or Jesus. They have miserable life, full of punk, full of pain and pointless brain which they don't use. What's the thing I am trying to tell you about? Hmm. Lets see. God is every where, he's in you, he's out side of you. His everywhere where you look, go out side and go into a lovely park. You will see trees, birds and nature or even look at the stars at night. This is God. And now go into a town, pay your bills and go to work, this is it, you are on the devils side, the matrix side.

Devil make you work for the money if you are not aware, he will make you drink alcohol, have sex, addict you from others and he will tell you lies, just like on tv. This is the Ego, I was talking about. On devils side you are wasted, your life is done, finished. On Gods side you are free, you are enlighten and understand that life has a special meaning FOR YOU! Religion doesn't tell you this. I do! Why so many wars has been created because of religion differences? First of all it based on the past, as the religion had to start off somewhere. The differences between of people and different mind setting are the other thing, which lead to hater-ism of two different religions. Now, what's the problem? The problem of your life is religion and it has been for many thousands of years. You have different groups, different people believing something different. Religion has been created to manipulate people, gain money, power and make limits on the public. They don't tell you exactly what God wanted to tell us in reality, they just change it according to the Government Policies.

In fact Jesus wanted us to live in peace and being part of a one big society. He wanted us to appreciate each other, but something is wrong right? Do you still don't believe wrong, bad, sad, furious behaviours. The people acting this way have something wrong in their minds, they have been strictly manipulated in their own thoughts. That is why they are acting so dumb and wrong. Devil is too strong, but Gods love is much stronger. Open your eyes and see the world around you, get away from your illusions, money, fame wanting and power gaining, and develop your self in this moment. Your moment is creating your reality and that's what Jesus said in his teachings. It just takes to say "thank you" after an argument, good conversation, appreciation of time or place, after competing yourself to something impossible and achieving. "Thank you" these are the important words that you give to universe. Universe will give the same situation back in a different form or circumstances. That's how God react to our life's. If your life is a flow to waste your time in trying to get rich working for the same business over 4 or even 9 years then you in a bad spot. Nothing will change, but if something will change then this could be a loss of your job.

Then you will be surprised that really you don't own anything. You just are getting addicted to things you have, so forget what you have right now, not physically but mentally. You will see that nothing belongs to you and you are one spiritually amazing thing that is totally free. Religion is very manipulative, it works closely with illuminati which has a lot of different symbolisms which are making the real you unknown. People are avoiding each other, why? Everybody is sick, everybody has something wrong with their thinking, there are really few people who think straight, and these people are totally enlighten and real Gods followers. People are controlled by beast, in our life this is European Union which is creating all of money, new schooling systems and making people totally dumb. Everyone should be in a psychiatric place, but there is so many of us that we really are enslaved and that's why we have all these jobs being created. World is sick, and only way to see that is to drop illusions, and making your vision cleared. Practice the real God and not fake beast follower such as famous musical industry artist, best actor of the year, somebody rich or wealthy, but look only at your self. Define what you need in your life.

Jesus was the messiah who said that God is the only way to freedom and do not listen to people who say differently. All of these physicians or scientists believe only in their own work, trying to prove that Jesus wasn't the only Lord. Maybe they are right. Jesus came on this earth as an average person does, but did everyone know these things of Jesus Christ was Teaching? Of course there might be some people that Jesus might meet on his way before he was teaching, that knew the truth. Jesus is Son of God as only he was able to heal by touch and only he has been the one who was crucified still believing in the only God. Jesus is Son of God just like everyone else, and his still on this planet, just like you are too! Referring to Scientists and religions that do not believe in Jesus as the Lord, most of these people believe different stories and theories but don't listen to the real truth. They are all based on the system (devils work) to prove that God doesn't exist, only to make us to fear pointless life. This is when Satan is taking over peoples lives. Son of God, Jesus came onto our earth as a messenger of the truth, of life, sense of life and God himself. He has been created as a human who can look like us, teach like us, speak like we are speaking to turn his messages in people towards God. At the beginning of your life, you have never been told to whom God you are preaching or believing in. What if you have been born in Catholic Home and you went to church everyday, if you don't believe in God or god then to whom you are praying to? Remember that if you don't have a Lord God in your mind when you pray, you won't even notice that your prayer will impact the Satan side of religion, with high benefit. This will influence your life in a negative way but only for a short period of time before you start to sin. You will loose yourself and your whole awareness. You will become another sheep. You are one anyway. Start working on your self!

Jesus showed you the way, just let your soul to be with him and he will help you along the way.

New world and predictions

Beast is everywhere, and people who really see this in our world do understand this. See all of the really worsen situation of the world are being treated as strange and psychologically sick by other people who don't really see that. This is good or bad? People who are trying to make world better are being treated unfair and are being put into prisons for a better purpose to enslave more people than we have. OPEN YOUR EYES. New world is being made to enslave population, to get rid of many billions of people, to make us feel bad about our selves, to manipulate the real you, to make you feel like you are nothing when you are alone, to stop your life being dependent on you own way. Realise this now that we haven't have our own life, you are working to make the dream of the new world order coming true, this dream is to kill out a person just like you are. The predictions are not longer predictions. They are true and more people realised this. What can we do? We need to fight against devil the beast.

This is not clear but anti-christ is alive and he will do anything to get rid of our positiveness. World has been different 6000 years ago. Then people were free, they had to do what ever they needed to do. What about these days? GO TO WORK! Go to school! Get out of my house! Don't touch me! F*** off! People by opening their own businesses enslave the people. The government is making us dumb by making us work, to feel depressed, so we need drugs or technology to feel better, through which the money has been generating. Some of these people doesn't have a clue what to do with their money, they earn it so much. Look how many rivers and lakes are intoxicated, cutting off trees and woods to build new cities. There is a lot of different predictions and all of them have to be proven right or wrong. Some of them just exist and others are imagination of somebody's mind. How do we see are world? Just look deep inside your head and open imagination. This will totally show you how you look on to life when you open your eyes. This experiment will only work the understanding definitely is based on things as they are. Strange? I know it sound strange. Because you hang around with people without brains, your life becomes exactly the way that other people have created out of you. You need and this is necessary to be your self no matter what. In order to find the true real you, you will need to sacrifice everything and feel depressed. That's the only way to get mad, to start doing something. Do not allow anyone or anything to get in your way, fight a way and follow as a champion! Every decision you make, you believe, every mistake you make you fail to learn new skill. Failure doesn't mean you are lost and defeated! You fall to get back up even stronger! Remeber!

Illumination of the Mind

Illumination = Light, enlightened, lightened

People don't understand this word. If the mind is illuminated it interacts with the brain to create an illusion in reaction of our movement. This will mean that if we are created from atoms and they match together while we think, it has a power to change things and your world altogether everywhere. Things are more illuminated to an illusion which we create in our eyes and to our believe systems. If the physics have discovered an ideal theory of things matching together, and it has been proven that without a matter if the two objects are away from each other or very close together, they still match like a one object in relation to two different objects. This is called officially quantum physics. So, if the mind is creating your reality why the heck you haven't got what you want? How do the mind work? Mind is a very mysterious place, it has everything and nothing at all. Referring back to quantum physics, we can make sure that thought is related with the brain, your brain transmits all of the information and the mind is showing you the thoughts of curiosity, answers and questions. This is all what mind is about. If mind is manipulated it will create a reaction in the thinking process, which could or will lead to different thought and so on. The only difference is that the thought doesn't have to be completely right, or it could be totally wrong as the mind has wrong information. Think about this before you watch Television, play games or even listen to music. As theory has been proven that world has leaders, and these people are manipulating our minds to keep us to be as far from the truth, they carry on treating you as a sheep to generate their money. They keep us away from the truest potential of our reality, and your life.

Think about your favourite song, and analyse the real meaning of this song you are thinking about. You will see which type of programming and manipulation it has on your brain. This will mean that people are actually not stupid, but dumbed in the way of thinking. Look at different illusions which are existing right now in your mind. So why don't you have what you always wanted? That is only because if you have an illusion in the brain and it has a bad transmission to your mind, this generates wrong thoughts. Thoughts are creating your life. Everything you see is a thought. Thoughts in which you give things their real meaning, are generating a power which spread into universe. If you have a bad month and you will drown into a bad habit of thinking of your life as a failure, what will happen at the end of the month? You will feel even more sad and depressed than you have been. Things are always always O.K. It takes a lot of bad thoughts to make you fall behind with your life and kill your dreams. So, try to avoid information of any kind, live in the existence as here and now. Feel good as this is the only way to communicate with God and the universe. Think good to communicate with the universe and ask Jesus for what you want in your life. I would recommend spirituality and enlightenment. Illusion of the mind has lots of of meanings. In the spirituality world you believe and know of God and evil. If quantum physics prove that we have soul, then this means that ghosts, and God is real. Just feel this life, stop thinking, let it be, be natural!

Motivation Part

Think of your life right now and look for what you want out of it. You need to find your self first. You need to know what you know and how you will use it to create a new thought to make your life a goal, related meaningful mission, than just sit and think of what you could of done. Try to see your life as an experiment. Go to people and ask them questions as an experiment. Go and do something you always wanted as an experiment. Set yourself a task and hold on to it firmly, do everything you can to reach a point in which you will know that you life is extremely meaningful. The experiment will show if you are living your illusions, if you are afraid of certain things, how do you look at certain things, is it good or bad? You can do what ever you want in your life. Just decide who you want to be. This is the main reason why I'm writing this book. I'm experimenting my self, if my work and knowledge has any meaning to other peoples life's. My purpose is to help you understand your life, as many people are afraid that life doesn't move forward at all these people are right. Life doesn't move at all only, if you don't move or develop your self. Practice awareness, practice experimentation of your life and remember that this is only an experiment, so you don't have to feel guilty or bad if things go wrong. Good luck, stay strong, become a warrior out of your own failures. You don't like your friends or employers, so why are you still with them. You are keeping with a group of failures, you will or have become a failure your self. Get unattached, create new path only for yourslef. Don't talk about it with no body else, keep it to your self and work day in and day out.

The meaning of life and seeking purposes

How many times people are talking about life in a bad way, miserable and they don't do nothing about it. Why do you do this to your self anyway? Life has a meaning if you have thoughts. You have thoughts so, try to show and prove to your self that your thoughts are right to what you want to feel. As I said before, only you can create your own reality. And aim small and imperfect to make it big and it doesn't have to be perfect. Just do what you know or positively think is good for you. Do not listen to other people! They will tell you that whatever you want to ACCOMPLISH is IMPOSSIBLE! These people are asses, and if you believe them you won't even try. The best way to change your self is to keep your life to your self. Only for the time when you will try to change your circumstances. It is hard to change life in one day, this means you need to create a mind setting and discipline which will allow you to do whatever you love everyday, no matter how hard it will be. Yes! Do things that need to be done only because you CAN do them, don't do anything because you NEED to. It is only thing to change your life to become better everyday. Yes! Exactly!

Talk to your self and seek purpose of your life and find out what's important to you. But only to you. Not your mother, not your father, not sister, friends or any one else who could tell you how to do it. Be your self all the time once you have found the truest you! I! Then you will be able to say what ever you want and without being forced to do anything at any time by nobody. You will decide how you spend your time in your life, you will decide what's the real meaning of your life is. You can have a life without mind as well, how do birds life and other animals? They don't have a mind or thinking skill, only intuition. They have totally natural life. Humans the only important creation of our universe on our planet are able to speak, think, visualise, and create new existence to a mind of your own path. Path should choose you. But if you have no idea what you want, mostly because of fear then this is necessary to become your self first with true understatement of our natural world. Be nobody, think and visualize of your future, live and work in present time.

I don't know what is your own goal, but I know that it is possible no matter what. We really need to give everything into our thinking to understand that there is something we can do in our lives. What would you feel if you succeed at something you love? What do you like doing about your life when you are not working? What's the things that drives you to understand all new level of your existence. Do you understand that our life is a matrix, its really generated programme which will actually make you feel like everything is real. Strange and hard to believe it, right. Science has made everything to show that our life has something to give, but first we need to invest your thoughts and mind. Keep on trying and never give up.

Never give up! Why. I have found out that if you are doing something all the time and suddenly you get hard moments. These moments, or moment will make you think negatively about your self. And once you stop and give up, your life will stop. When you give up something, your life stop. If you had been working on your dream for a long time, your dream will cost you 6 months or 1 year if you give up at any time. But if you keep going, no matter what, you will become a rock and nobody will be able to move you out of your track. If you simply think of your life as it's bad and not great. It will become negative and your own mind will destroy you through thoughts. Discipline is everything, mind setting and learning new skills.

Thoughts and the projector

This is important to understand everything about your own thoughts. The reason for this is because thoughts you have are creating your life. How do you feel good? Think of something good, funny or something you feel appreciation for. Yes it's true. If you say "thank you" everyday and it doesn't matter what happened already or what will happen, feel and be here now. People don't understand what's the difference between past and future.

The past is a good session, your past defined you, your past created this person you are right now. Whatever you have done before in the past, your life has been created in a way to show you as you are right now. How does this work? Think of what will happen to you in the future. Think and write it on a paper. Once you have written this on a piece of paper you will realize that life is simply about creating. What ever you wrote down, you have created it through your thoughts and the mind setting you have in your brain. Can you see your power? You are wonderful being, you are nothing and you are everything. People think that they are nobody, that people with fame and money become that way by lack. No! If you create your future by your thoughts, you will change your mentality even without knowing about it. Purpose of our life is simply, thought and willingness to grow spirituality.

Although you can always choose if you want to have a life that have a meaning or you just settle down and waste life working. I am not letting my self down. I am going to work on my self everyday from now. I am healthy. I am the best. I am great and I am powerful. I have everything that I should have at this very moment. I am beautiful. I am lucky. While you read my book, you changing your mind setting. You need to understand, that your life has a value when you say those two easy words. You will see and experience a different ways for your life. I am confident. I am lovely. I am the best person I could be. What are these words? The answer is "I am". Two most powerful words in the whole universe.

Your life divides in to ME and I AM. Me is not powerful, but I am is most powerful. But if you find out a way to join these two together. Your life will change not only dramatically but you will find out that life is totally fine and it has a lot to give. Once you are aware, you just only ask once and believe. One day whatever you have asked for, it will come.

What ever you feel you will project through your eyes. Your life is something of a 3D creation. You see a programme out of an atoms, out of a light. We are something big. I am the opportunity. Think of what you want in your mind, visualize and see things as if you have them in this moment. Soon you will find out a way to get things you want. It is impossible that I can't grow better. If you say that you cannot do something, you are right. If you say you can do something, you are right as well. I am aware of my soul. Remember about your soul, you have really big power. What ever you want to see and you are willing to sacrifice things, you will receive instead.

What do you want out of your life now?

Now you are able to say who you really are. Well, maybe not yet but I know one. You are waking up. You are experiencing new reality from now. I am happy for you. I am simply happy for everything that is happening to my and your life. I am me. You are new person. I am new existence. I am a champion. I am aware that I am a champion. I am the best. I am number one. I am number one. I am winning. I am me. I am lovingness. I am world. I am a part of the creation and the celebration of love. I am aware that the control system is not in control of me. I am great. I am amazing. I am AMAZING! I am my self. I am presence. I am perfect. I am aware that I am the creator. I am the positive result of love. I am in control of my self. I am always looking forward. I am always observing. I am learning. I am aware that I am my self. I am a receiver. I am the reason I am alive. I am believing in success. I am always giving, I am always receiving. I am my mind. I am vibrating success.

I love my life, neither what happens. I know I have my own I path. Everything I see is coming from me. God loves me. I am experiencing love from God. I am in love with my self. I am the opportunity. I am light. I am aware of all good in my life. Do you understand?

Become yourself, start separating yourself from the society who doesn't give you anything back. People who are making you sick, people who are not loving you the way you are. I am the best person in the universe. How do I know? Because God gave me life. I am here. I am aware that my life is something better than before. I am my moment. I am now. You need to love your self. With love you will find things you love. With love you will become free of obligations, free of complications, free of problems, aware of your own destiny. I am perfect. But if you want to go out there and look at your life from the other side of your moment, you will find your purpose. I am power. I will not stop reaching my goals until my heart is beating. I will not stop reaching my goals until we have sunshine at day, and moonlight at night. I am changing the world. I am aware that I am accomplishing my life desires.

I want you to start doing something you never experienced. Before you do that, you will need to prepare. You need to stop growing on your negativity, so get off your tv or computer and sell it. Get rid of everything that is making you sick around your house. For the money earned from these things, get a membership with the local gym. Start working on your self. You are here, you need to understand that you need to do something in order to reach your LIFE, not GOAL. Stop being afraid because of somebody said you cannot do it. You are of your own, you are not that person who made you look stupid or dumb. Your mind is of your own, your mind is not public. I am strength. I am beautiful. I am influencing people around. I am alive.

Why are we alive?

God created you to have your own dreams, to imagine, to be his light, to be his son or daughter, to give you experiences of world and its beautiful nature. Beast changed everything that we call nature. Our aim is to create naturalized world once again, we are Gods shining stars.

Everyone is important. Everyone need to know this. People don't want to know this. They describe it as stupidity. These people are addicted to the system and they do not live their own thoughts, they feel and live the government thoughts. Every day you need to work on your dream, but first you need to decide who you want to become!

What is the problem? Me is an ass, you are an ass. These should be no problem at all. People are sick minded. But never try to change them, never. What you should do. You start with a person you see in the mirror. You tell him that you commit to start growing, learning and becoming your future. It doesn't matter what your name is.

Doesn't matter who you are. Doesn't how you think of your self. It even don't matter how old you are. You need to know only that you are powerful and you can change people around your self, when you have changed. When you change, you change your behaviour, you make something out of nothing in the universe. You are going to be something great. Try not to look at your success but only see who you will become after the adventure. You are writing a complete new story and you have the best live experiences to start and create what ever you want.

You need to be in control of your self. You need to look forward, not your past because it doesn't exist. You should be the reason you are happy and smile. You are yourself. Get busy, because we have a lot to do. First of all, sacrifice things you are addicted to, clear your mind out of any obstacles. God created you, he embodied your soul into your body to show you the life we have here. Do you see what I am saying? Pay attention. God has a quest for you, this quest is to love others and most importatly finding the truest you; the will to change your life and people around you. Never attempt to change anyone, unless you are enlightened enough and whoever this person is, is willing to change their life too. If they don't want to change, just leave them in Gods hands and carry on doing what ever you can go get to your dreams! If you don't, you will not only feel bad and dissapointed with yourself but, what will happen to the people around you? Answer is in you.

How badly do you want something? You need to define exactly how much work you will give in it. If it is a minimum you are wrong but, also anything is good. Only because wrong doesn't exist.

You are the light that world needs

Everything you see is light once you are the light. Also, you can spot darkness. You need to feel relaxed in any situation because life is about you. Imagine your self somewhere where you want to be. Where you wish to be. Feel like you don't have a name, you don't answer or make excuses. You are just here. You need to separate your self from the system, the matrix. People who are working all of their lives in a average level, they are wasting their life decreasing their attention to details. Waste of life to pay checks. This is not real life. Once you are the feeling power and can reflect on your own successful thoughts, you will understand everything. You are nothing and everything. Do you know the law of attraction? No? Seek truth within you. If you had argument with somebody, you need to forgive them. Just forgive your self first. Get off negativity, your mind will open to new opportunities. Life is everything, life is universe, life is planets, life is you, life is me, I am life. Don't look for God, his here already. Be focused on your goals if you know what they are. You need to be focused every single day on what you want to achieve. I don't care how many failures I went through I want more because I learn from them. On day, one day its is going to be my day. I want to change the world. But think about yourself first and you will see how things will change around you. Don't be discouraged by a bad day, bad week, bad month or bad year, keep on doing what you wanted to do and what you really love. If you are still not on this stage yet then you need to fight. It's hard. I know. But if you need a change in your life and you see it, you will need to start somewhere. Start small, even on things that don't mean to you anything. That will change over time, and you'll be better and better every single day. Take those classes, go for a job, run 3 miles, go to the gym, go swimming, learn maths, learn how to do something you don't know and learn from mistakes. Read a book or listen to some motivational videos, these will change your thoughts, these will change your mentality, you will change your life. Don't think, but feel. Be great. Be the best you can be. You are the light the world needs. Work on your self, one day you will become free, you will change the world. How? Work on your self, know your self first. Don't moan, complain, keep it simple, don't listen to somebody who is a failure and doesn't do anything about it. You are your own. No body can do anything for you in your lifetime. But remember that you are limitless, but time is limited. Your life is ending even now. Everyday you are much closer until you are dead. So, what you need to do? This is simple too. With your mind, go into the future. Imagine you are on your death bed. Think about what you could of done in the past. The past you thinking about is now, this very moment. You can change your life and circumstances. If world is negative you think negatively, right? Yes, this is right. But really have a go and think how would you feel and think of yourself after doing something you believe in and deep in your heart know it's possible. Don't do it for anybody else, do it you yourself. You think this is selfish? Then you are wrong. Why? Because when you get where you need to be, you will be able to do anything. Anything includes also, a change in the world. All of these things comes to one definition. How badly do you want to make your dream reality? Ask your self that and feel it, believe it, work on it and develop.

Development of a mental Voice

Start talking to your self in a positive way as it will be the only thing you will ever hear to be positive! DO NOT EXPECT anybody else to tell you are something! If you count, count on your self! Thi will help you reaching your goal. See yourself as a champion, bold with charisma and without fear. Be strong and hard to any situations that might be around. You are in control of your life, people fear you and you know what you are going for! The mental system of our minds is so strong that if we don't reproggrame our subcontious mind we will fall down and won't be able to get up! Ever. I am hard enough to reach my truest dreams, no matter what they will talk about me, what they will say. Haters have their Job, this is their job to tell you that you are not enough. Wake up to this world and see things as there are. The nature, the real meaning for the words and what people are talking to you about! You are bilind to normal things. Its time we see it cleary, to be positive and totally free of obligations. You are your own and DO NOT EVER FORGET IT!

The comfort Zone

How do you feel and think about your life? Think. How many times you have been afraid of different things around your life? Fear is outside the comfort zone. If you don't tackle it, then it will gain power over you. Don't be a soft individual. Become hard enough to go through whatever needs to be done. Play this game as never before. Get you health up, endurance, fitness, develop new skills, read books, eat healthy, stop smoking, get out there and find the real you, you are the person who is the most important right now. But you're soft, lazy, looser and boring. Or maybe you hard, confident, wealthy and healthy. Think how to tackle the comfort zone every day. Learn how to play life as a game. The only thing you have is your mentality, right? If you don't proceed to get better, your day will never show up. At least try, and be ready to fail. Failure is another success. Once you understand that when you fail you will be able to say that you did something you were afraid of. But you are stronger now, and you're not afraid of this any more.

Once you get on track of your purpose, when you find out that your dream is true you will not be in fear any more. But you matter, and you can do anything you want. Life is about pursuit of your own happiness. If you are happy in average and you are not doing anything to change your life, you are wasting it. Money, bills, girls, or men, problems and worrying doesn't give you nothing, all of these stops at one point of your life. You stop enjoying it. But do something you love, do something that you feel good about and keep on working on your dream. If for any reason you don't have a dream then just find it. Decide who you want to become, you might be right or you might be wrong. Do it anyway, and the real you will start coming to existence. You will be alive and ready for more pain, more failure, more problems and once you fight the way through this battle you will see something you never experienced before. Start with what you have, it doesn't matter what's your situation. Become a Champion, a unbeatable rock, stand still and smile at all your problems. Trust me, one day it will fade away. Don't do it for me. Do it for you!! No matter what happened in your life!!! YOU MATTER!!!!! GET BUSY!!!

God will be with you all the time, he will help you. He will be with you when ever things get hard. We were all created to be, we were born to dream, we are all here to be strong. All our life is about fight, so make sure that you fight with light in your heart against evil. Believe in your dream first, then it will show up and you will see it finally, **not the other way**!

Expectations

Lets look at the expectations you have, your life is worth living? Isn't it? If you're expecting to get somewhere, that's good, really good. Aim high. But if you expect something from others, you in a trap. People make excuses and discourage you to get where you want to be. This is good as well. Why? People are in deep fear of things that they never tried out, the fear is overtaking them so They won't be able to move forward. Don't expect anything from these people as these people are failures and you by being in their area, will become one of them! Keep on working by your self, search for people from whom you could learn new skills. This is the way you have to be in order to be successful. Although don't get rid of failure people from your life totally. You need them on the way. The reason being are the complains, moans and discourages. Normally when you tell people who you want to become, they'll laugh and make jokes about you. You need that, because you get angry. They will make you feel bad, this is great. When that situation comes you need to feel good with your self. You get angry, so you be stronger. They will tell you what you can't do because it's impossible. Are you kidding me? What is impossible for you? The answer is nothing. You can do anything and this kind of expectation you should have in your mind all the time. Throw high, Shoot High! Get ready, you are on a way to reach you truest potential! Get busy. Drop all expectations from others and all of them that you expect.

-Life, in its true colours is worth living.

-Even when life isn't in its true colours, it is still worth living.

-Why?

- Becuase unawareness is a life in which you can

still wake up and live free of attachments.

- It only depends on your thoughts and Actions.

Twisted and Imagined ending

- This is so... so, funny how these people write books like this one. And they don't have a clue about anything that goes around our life. Robert Said.

- Stop, moaning, can't you see that everything that you wrote in this book was and is right? Sam cried.

- What?!! Robert Cried.

- Exactly!!

- How did this happened? I cannot remember anything, what do you mean, I have done all of this?

- I knew that you are sick and won't remember. I made you do it.

- But, how would you know what I went through, we only just met on taxi driveway. Robert started shaking.

- Are you sure that you are right? No!! We have met few days ago, why would you think that? Sam Asked.

- I can remember your yellow coat with a big blue umbrella, it was raining so heavily. Robert Cried out.

- Can you remember a black car with a woman and child inside? Can you??!!

- Yesss!!

- That was your wife and your son, you have totally forgot about them right? Sam Asked.

- What happened to me, why am I homeless living in a shelter than in my house. Robert thinking.

- Hey man, I am talking to you asshole.

- Um. -Robert is confused and starts to cry. -No, I don't know what happened to them!!

- I am sure you are able to remember this, it is important to know!! - Sam Cried with a smart voice.

- Keep away from me, do not ever show up again in my life!! - Robert started to tear up.

- I cannot leave you, that is not possible!

-Why, just go and leave me. Now!!!

- Ok, allright, I go but do not regret your decision.

- Why people are so dumb, I've just met him and his already started to make me feel like I'm nothing! But Sam is right, what happened to my Wife and my only Son? (Roberts mind started to thing backwards)

It is rainy Saturday Morning, and as usual I was about to get out of my house into the taxi to go at my boring and hatred job. Once again. I don't know how did this happened, but I got there in no time while reading the book I just brought called "Hope, the great Philosophy". I don't know what happened to me, I changed after this book. I understand so much even after few pages. But, what happened to me? I started to hate my job even more, I want to quit but if I quit I will loose employment and I won't get anywhere in life. Or do I? I went to work, when I arrived by the door of this restaurant. My name is Robert,

I am a Chef in the stupid restaurant where nothing changes, people see everything differently in the same place with the same circumstances. I don't understand, is it me who is sick minded or them? Is it strange to be stuck in the same timing or situation and it doesn't matter what day it is, everyday seems the same. Same dishes, few changes but its not a change at all, me talking to people in different way, I am totally dead, I feel like I am dying, My job is making me sick. That's what I think about in my work, I am stuck in a system which doesn't work, so what am I supposed to do?

After whole day of thinking of my job being so bad and I wish it could be doing something I love to do. But what do I love to do? This is a good question. Finally the clock showed up at ten o clock evening, and after busy day, the taxi was waiting for me already, as usual. I got changed quickly and went out to the taxi, and there was a man standing beside the taxi.

- Hey man, hurry up because I'm late already. -This man said with a convincing voice.

- Ok – I said while holding this book in my hand.

- I wanted to introduce my self, and my name is Sam, but who are you? - Sam asked.

- My name is Robert, and can I ask you what are you doing here? - I asked

- It doesn't matter...

The driver looked at me sitting on the back of the taxi with this guy talking to me. Although taxi driver looked only at me.

- Pegasus Drive please, Sir.

- Ok – he answered whilst whispering swear words.

I have not heard what the driver said because of this guy, he was talking and talking and talking.

- I wanted to tell you something about universe, did you know that UFO's exist and there was actual conspiracies saying people in the past had a direct touch with them. - Sam continued...

-What you mean a touch? - I asked to make him stop talking.

- Come with me to a pub, we have a drink and we will talk.

- No, I need to go home. - I said.

The driver answered - I think you had a long day today. You asked me to go at the Pegasus Drive not to Millway Road, Sir. -The driver replied.

The driver was right. Why did I say the drive road of the pub, that I go to sometimes instead of my home road. - I was thinking again.

- I think you are tired, man. Take a day off tomorrow and come with me, I will show you how to live life. - Sam said with convincing voice once again.

Somehow I didn't know what am I doing no more. I just said yes, when I though something was wrong. I didn't care any more. I am just tired. So, tired of work of life and of anything getting in my way. I think that Sam could be my first friend ever. I even forgot about my jobs notice. I gave it 5 days ago, tomorrow is termination of my employment. How did this happened, I don't understand how did something like that could potentially happened. I know only one thing. Everything that is happening in my life, it was created by me according to the book. How is my life depended on me by hundred percent. It doesn't matter, things are happening and I have no control over it so why should I even care? I felt a taste of cold beer on my lips, that was like a nice dream. How did I get here so quickly?

- Do you like it? - Sam asked.

-Yeah man, thank you for this. I feel like I really needed it. - I answered.

I was about to ask him how did I get there so quickly. Somehow I forgot whole way up here, like if I wasn't even in that taxi at all.

-How can I help you bro? - He asked.

- Sorry, what you mean. I never wanted anything thing from you. - I replied.

- What you mean? At the taxi you said you wanted some of the pills I have. -He said.

- What pills? Have I took any of them at the taxi? I can't remember. - I got stressed.

- No, you haven't took any yet, but you asked me if I got something to make you feel better. - Sam said.

- Well, I cannot remember but yes, I need help. I hate my job, I hate everything I touch. -I replied.

- Really, but you look like you have everything. Do you really thing this is pointless? - He asked.

-No, I know what I need but I don't have courage to do this. - I replied.

- Anyway, I won't tell you anything else. But, I have a big case to tell you about. - He said.

- Allright, what is it? - I asked.

- Never, ever talk about me. My life has been manipulated in many ways and I don't want anybody to talk about me. You see me, and only you can know about me. Right? - he said very seriously.

- Yeah, ok that's totally fine. - I replied.

- Ok then, cool. Finish your beer and lets go in town. - He said.

- I have a question. I said.

- Yes? - Asked.

- What kind of book do you read? I see this book in your pocket. - I asked.

- Oh, sorry. Yeah, this book is yours. I kept it for you. - He answered.

- Thank you. - I said without even knowing I had a book.

- Lets go man, no time to waste. - He said.

Sam has been the great guy, smart and totally intelligent. His face is bruised but, the blue suit he is wearing it shiny and glamorous. After he said that, I lost it again. I didn't know what I am doing, who I am. Did he lie to me? He actually gave me those pills, and I drunk that beer. I feel it on my stomach. Suddenly I woke up.

- (Oh I feel so bad, and I will be sick) I thought to my self. I cannot open my eyes yet, where am I? I asked.

-This is my house bro. - This voice said, fading away.

- Ah, Sam. - Where am I? - Still trying to open my eyes.

- No where, you don't exist. - He said.

I got stressed again and fear over helmed me once again, I woke up in no time.

- Hey, who are you girl?! - I asked this girl sleeping next to me. I cannot remember anything.

I smelled something disgusting in the air, so I grabbed this girl to ask her again.

- Now, tell me who are you? - Now I grabbed her hand and pulled
  towards me.

Her head flipped on to my side, and once I saw her sticking out skull
on her face, I woke up once again.

- God, please help me. What is going on with me? - Whispered.

I woke up by a bin under my house, and it was also raining. There was
something in the bin smelling so bad that I literally needed to get sick
on purpose.

- Where Am I going with my life? What's the purpose, everything is
  so shit and it is even more disgusting. Life is so hard and I have got
  enough. I want to commit suicide. I'm wet, covered in some trash,
  freaking life is so hard. - I was moaning, and crying my eyes out.

- I got up very slowly and in a depressed mood started to make small
  steps towards my house.

My thoughts started to bring me different ideas from last night. I didn't
remember anything at all. I raised my head when my mind started to
think about work. Overwhelmed with all of my stupid stress, I needed
to get to work. Now. Oh, no.

- I got my key out of my pocket and went up to the door, picking the book which was left on the step just before the door. I went inside, went to a quick shower, got my self ready and checked the time.

- It's already seven o clock in the morning, I got two hours before I get there. That's good. I can't even remember when I was carrying on to read that book, sat on the sofa. I didn't want food, drink or anything. I wanted to read. Somehow I believed that there is something in that book to change my life over.

- "Sadness, happiness, lovingness, fears, disappointment, aggressiveness, fake you.

I woke up once again, with tears in my eyes. What can I do to stop thinking and start doing? I have read lots of different books, I have been preparing for this time to change my life all over again. But, again I've woke up crying to the pillow and cannot do anything with my life, I am alone. Nobody understands me, and I don't understand anybody. How can you live your life with being a fake person." - Read. This verse seems just like me. But what does he mean about an fake person? I am not fake, I am me. I have my own life, I can't be fake. Although, maybe I am fake, I am an idiot which believes in something that doesn't exist.

- HAHAHA – I started laughing, but in heart I had enough. I didn't want to go to work.

- I called taxi over again – Calling on their number. And for a second I forgot who I am again.

- After 5 Mins whilst waiting for the taxi. I saw this car, this little Ferrari owned by Sam. - I watched with amazement.

Once he opened his door of his car, and he took his head out I got really nervous.

- Hey you fucking prick, what happened last night? Why did you leave me under them bins? - I was so angry.

- Calm down, and remember about our agreement. - he answers while chewing a gum. - Calm down and get in the car – he continued.

I got in the car and I lost it again. It feeling like I am sleeping, I don't know what is going on, I don't know if I am alive or even I do not hear anything too. How does this happened?

- Accidentally I have been tapped few times by the taxi driver, I didn't know what am I doing again. But, I was under the works front door again.

- Sorry, Sir. And thank you, how much do I own? - I asked.

- Sir, You have already paid. Are you ok? - He answered.

- Aha. - I left the taxi and slowly went inside the restaurant.

Again, I can see all of these smiles send towards me. I have enough of these people being so kind and nice to me, you can get sick. You do something wrong, they say that everything's alright. People without meaning, without purpose. They are living only to make this stupid system to work, it is not even a good thing for them but, the system and the money.

- How are you today Robert? - One of the staff asked.

- Come here! - I said to this guy. And once he came over I went insane.

- Can you stop talking to me in this type of way? Can you stop asking me if I am ok, could you? I have got enough of being asked the same question over and over again. If I will be feeling bad I would end up in a hospital or even not come into work you idiot. But, no I am not ok. This type of people are the only a cancer to this world, yes, I am talking about you. - I replied, with aggressiveness.

- Ok, sorry man. - He replied.

I felt like I am getting my real life back. I started to feel bad against the people but, good with my self again. But, I still need to learn how to control my thoughts.

- I see it already. - I said to myself.

My life has been totally controlled by something or someone. This thing that didn't allow me to sleep, didn't allow me to feel alive, didn't allow me to live, I was dead. Satan is doing good job in making people feel ""Sadness, happiness, lovingness, fears, disappointment, aggressiveness, fake ness"", and only to his own benefit.

But where is Sam?

His alive, me is Dead, but I got reborn. I am awake. I just let it go.

- I was the evil one, and he showed me the way. I was the real ego, and he showed me life. Ego was my attachment, the attitude changed drastically after I meet him. Satan is the Ego and he is working his way over my mind all the time. He is not dead, but I kill him slowly through my mind. He is in my mind, I kill him by doing things that I never did before. I don't need money, fear, darkness, happiness, confidence, greed, grateful life because I AM NOT MY EGO. I AM HERE BECUASE I HAVE OPPURTUNITY TO BE MY SELF, nothing at all, exactly just like you are. If people try to convince you to their own lies, they are not fooling anybody else but them selves, living fake life. Defeting the ego will stop opinions, judgement, fear and could make you happy the way you are, not the way that society created you of.

I had it all wrong, living the unaware life.

Live Productive Life

"Be warned" will kill your dreams, as you will become more and more cautious. This is not the way to be. Don't try but, act like you are new person, totally new with new behaviour, without ego. Don't judge other people, "be warned" as they will start judging you. You won't be happy about that at all. Keep your life simple and adventorous. Get somewhere and have fun. Remember that you don't have to be at your job, you have decided to stay there. Just don't judge things you don't like, as it actaully helps you to create normal healthy approach that you can't buy. You can only learn. Pick a book and learn, but don't follow exactly what it says. Just learn and make your own mind once you have finished reading it. Get another book and read on, learning still. If you follow the second book, and it says something that you shouldn't believe in the first book you have read, you get ruined. So, don't follow anything in life, but instead become a student. Others don't need to know. Ask questions, change your behaviours, be calmer, have your own personality and be a life time student. You will learn more skills, so it doesn't mean that the problems will disapear. It only means that this will help you to work on your bad situation. Be productive too, set your life to higher purpose and act on your thoughts!

What do I mean to be productive?

Being productive is to consistently learn new skills, gain knowledge, change diet, get fit and change your mind setting. Create challenges for yourself, get successful in one or more parts of your life. Read books, as all the knowledge from the other people's past experience can be helpful. Help other people if they need somebody, you will make friends and you would help yourself to learn new skills, maybe even get new contacts or get into totally new situation. Don't even think how you will get it, just start with small things. And you will get surprised like things will change for you. But, remember that when you start this change, and you suddenlly stop after some time, you will already feel change. When you stop at any moment, this will normalize your learning and that would be your new way of being. But, what if you stop in a bad time, where everything went wrong. If you don't follow personal development all the time, you will become a follower once again. You'll be a sheep once again. Ask yourself, if you want to live this way, or maybe you want more that you could ever think of? Think and you be wise.

Remember, once you are aware, you are everything and nothing. You can have anything without attaching to it, so you will have a peaceful life. The only thing you need to do is becoming a student and keep on Learning. Once you master your mistakes and sitautions when everything went wrong, you will start to feel greatness.

Do not just read this book and say that you have everything it takes, to get somewhere you want to be at. Why? Because that's another lie. Do not lie to your self anymore. Talk your mind, see really where you stand, what situation you are in. Keep it to your self and never tell about your dreams to nobody else. I believe that if you ever tell your dreams to anybody, they will never come TRUE! Before you commit your first step, LOOK IN THE MIRROW AND SEE THE GREATNESS. Not the potential! If you have potential, that good. But, if you had the potential for many years then you wasting your talent only because you are not unleashing your potential any more! Show the world that you are here, show your self that you are the best version of yourself. If you read carefully this book then you know that this is not about making your self a fool, or a cool funny kid. You will become a warrior. Dream life to the fullest. Never give up, or give in. If you survived and just read this book until the end, you are the truest champion. Remember that your problems are not bigger than you are. Peoblems are only situations that can be always solved!

If you can't do anything, then Believe in your dream and it will show up one day. If nothing is working at all, then Just

HOPE

and work on your dream today and for ever!

I just wanted to inspire you, if I did good job doing it keep it to your self! Love your LIFE the way it is and start digging for more!

Printed in the United States
By Bookmasters